Hiring
and Firing

The Lessons Learned Series

Wondering how the most accomplished leaders from around the globe have tackled their toughest challenges? Now you can find out—with Lessons Learned. Concise and engaging, each volume in this new series offers twelve to fourteen insightful essays by top leaders in business, the public sector, and academia on the most pressing issues they've faced.

A crucial resource for today's busy executive, Lessons Learned gives you instant access to the wisdom and expertise of the world's most talented leaders.

Other books in the series:

Leading by Example
Managing Change
Managing Your Career
Managing Conflict
Starting a Business

Hiring
and Firing

LESSONS
Boston, Massachusetts

Copyright 2008 Fifty Lessons Limited
All rights reserved
Printed in the United States of America
12 11 10 09 08 5 4 3 2 1

Library of Congress Cataloging-in-Publication Data

Hiring and firing.
    p. cm. — (Lessons learned)
  ISBN 978-1-4221-2308-9
  1. Employee selection. 2. Employees—Dismissal of.
  HF5549.5.S38H567 2008
  658.3'112—dc22

                        2007038952

679331

In partnership with Fifty Lessons, a leading provider of digital media content,
Harvard Business School Press is pleased to
announce the launch of Lessons Learned,
a new book series that showcases the trusted
voices of the world's most experienced
leaders. Through the power of personal
storytelling, each book in this series pre-
sents the accumulated wisdom of some of
the world's best-known experts and offers
insights into how these individuals think,
approach new challenges, and use hard-won
lessons from experience to shape their leadership philosophies. Organized thematically
according to the topics at the top of managers' agendas—leadership, change management, entrepreneurship, innovation, and
strategy, to name a few—each book draws
from Fifty Lessons' extensive video library
of interviews with CEOs and other thought

A Note from the Publisher

leaders. Here, the world's leading senior executives, academics, and business thinkers speak directly and candidly about their triumphs and defeats. Taken together, these powerful stories offer the advice you'll need to take on tomorrow's challenges.

We invite you to join the conversation now. You'll find both new ways of looking at the world, and the tried-and-true advice you need to illuminate the path forward.

⊰ CONTENTS ⊱

1. Pamela Marrone
   **Hire People Who Share
   Your Values**   1

2. Lauren Flanagan
   **Recruit the Best People Inside
   and Outside Your Organization**   7

3. Colin Day
   **Do Your Due Diligence on
   Prospective Employers**   14

4. Nicola Horlick
   The Opera Singer   19

5. Sir Donald Cruickshank
   Recruit Talent, Not Experience   27

6. Laura Tyson
   **Populate Your Inner Circle
   with Experts**   32

Contents

7. Gerry Roche
   **The Long-Range View over
   Short-Term Expediency**   36

8. Jody Thompson and Cali Ressler
   **Focus on Retaining Talent,
   Not Hiring**   42

9. Sir Mark Weinberg
   Hire People with Integrity   50

10. Erroll Davis Jr.
    **Remove People Sooner
    Rather Than Later**   56

11. John Roberts
    How to Let People Go   62

12. Paul Anderson
    Don't Deliver Bad News Badly   69

13. Lord Sharman
    Letting People Go   75

14. Peter Ellwood
    Be Tough but Compassionate   79

About the Contributors   85
Acknowledgments   99

Hiring
and Firing

Hire People Who Share Your Values

Pamela Marrone

Founder and CEO, Marrone Organic Innovations

I MADE A LOT of mistakes on the hiring front in that I hired people who were technically competent and had the right industry background, but didn't actually have the same values that we in the founding team did. This had devastating consequences for everyone because they would go off in a direction that was different from what I might want. They actually didn't believe in the mission and the vision of the company, and were working countercurrent to what we wanted.

I'm talking to a lot of other entrepreneurs, and they have a similar problem in their companies. People come in, and they just want the job. They'll tell you what you want to hear, and then you find out they don't really believe in what you're doing. It's more common than you might think. So it's really important to have some kind of mechanism up front to find employees who're going to be aligned with you.

No one will be as passionate as you—the founder, the entrepreneur—but you want employees who are almost as passionate as you are about what you're doing. I hired some senior people—like a vice president of product development and a director of marketing—and they came in and spent the first six months trying to disprove our technology, because they had come from other companies that had competing technology. They had a hard time believing that our technology could possibly work as well as their technology in their old companies. They were quite disruptive because they would go over to the scientists and want to have them do all these experiments that would disprove how good our technology was.

This happened also with our salespeople. We'd hire salespeople from the industry; they were selling chemicals, and we were selling biological products, [which are] safer products that compete with chemicals and are a substitute for chemicals. So you want the farmer to use your biological, natural product instead of the chemical. We had some sales guys who were pitching our product to farmers, and they had to sell to the farmer our product as a substitute for a chemical pesticide. But they actually still believed that chemicals were better, even though our product was showing better yields and better-quality produce.

It is very difficult to run and grow a company when you have employees who are not aligned with what you're doing and what the mission and vision are. You have turnover, and you have to let employees go. It's very distracting and disruptive all around for all the employees. The key there was to, once you got them in the door, get them out quickly. But more important would be to screen them up front to ensure that they did have the values. That's not an easy task.

I actually was so paranoid after having a couple of misses that when I was hiring a new vice president of sales and marketing, I spent over three months trying every which way— [including] using a recruiter, who did some interviews, and ensuring that this person was going to be aligned. Even then, that one turned into not the outcome that I would have liked. I had to regroup and figure out what I was missing in the interview process.

I think I was still too focused on what the individuals could do for the company, instead of getting to those true values. So I started asking very different questions: Do you recycle? What kind of car do you drive? Do you eat organic food? And when you start getting to those life choices, then you would start finding the values. And you could tell if someone was faking, whether they recycled or not. That's how I could really flush out whether the employees were really believing in what we were doing.

In my new company that I'm starting, some of the founding team are suggesting that we have the value statement right out there up front. And we're actually going to make every employee sign it when we hire them. So it's a little different from just saying, "Yeah, yeah, yeah. I believe in it." When they actually have to sign it, then we can go back when we see someone not living up to those values and we can say, "Wait a minute. You signed this; you committed to this when you first started here. And we expect you to live by it."

TAKEAWAYS

⚔ Hiring individuals who are technically competent but do not share the values of the company's leaders can have devastating consequences.

⚔ It is extremely difficult to run and grow a company when employees aren't aligned with its mission because of the distractions and disruptions caused by turnover.

⚔ When hiring, screen individuals up front to ensure that they bring shared values. During an interview, ask questions that can flush out whether the person believes in what the company is doing.

⚔ Put your value statement up front, have new employees sign it, and tell them you expect them to live by it.

———◆———

Recruit the Best People Inside and Outside Your Organization

Lauren Flanagan

*Cofounder, and former CEO and Chairman,
WebWare Corp.*

———◆———

Hiring and Firing

IN MY OWN EXPERIENCES as a serial entrepreneur, in the many clients that we counsel at SCIO Corp., and in the companies who come to our angel fund, Phenomenelle Angels, the biggest issue that all the companies have isn't money—it's people. It's finding the right team.

It's very important in any venture that there's that entrepreneur with the passionate driving spirit who has this problem that they are compelled to solve. That's a critical ingredient. And they need relevant entrepreneurial and business experience—if not themselves, other members of the team.

What I see in many companies is a tendency, out of economy or whatever, not to get the best people, both inside and outside. Always having the best team inside and outside is essential. That means, day one, what's the best lawyer you can get for your business? Ideally, they're a national or global firm, so they can represent you in all the things that you want to do and bring credibility as well. What's the best accounting firm that you can bring in? And again, they don't have to be one of the biggest, but at least a large firm. And even if, out of economy, you can't afford a fully developed management team, what you can do is develop a world-class advisory board.

One of the companies we advise has a very thin management team, but they've put on Ben Cohen of Ben & Jerry's ice cream; John Whitehead, of Goldman Sachs; and one of the leaders in education. World-class members make up their advisory board. If you structure [the board] properly and make it interesting enough, it's possible to find outstanding, successful entrepreneurs who would like to be associated with your business. That's a really important thing to do.

Most people tend to hire people like themselves or people they're comfortable with. But that doesn't always bring the best management team. The best management team in young, emerging companies is one that is open and critical and, in fact, argumentative in many cases. They have disparate views, and they feel free to exchange them and discuss them and argue their points of view until either consensus is achieved or, if none can be reached, then the CEO will have to make a decision.

Then it's important that the management team fully supports that decision. That really has to be the rule—that you can say anything, and during the discussion and discovery phase all arguments are allowed; but once a decision is made, the whole team pulls behind the decision and gives 100 percent commitment. Persons that have the capacity to do that are essential. That means looking for people who are best for the skill set, who will work [in] the culture but might be very different. And that's a hard thing to do.

At WebWare, we had some interesting questions that we would ask at interviews after we went through all of them, to just try to find people who were interesting and interested in other things besides the work, because we found what tended to bring this critical thinking was a person, in general, who was exploratory about life. We would ask some really simple questions like, "We're taking you to a special lunch. It's a special occasion, and you can go anywhere. Where are we going, what are we going to eat, and who's with us?" There is really no wrong or right answer, but it told us a lot about how they thought, and even how they thought about answering that question. Not that it was a trick question; it was a question designed by its simplicity to see just how someone would answer.

We found that the really interesting people with the critical minds would say, "Well, anywhere in the world . . . Can we be on a mountaintop in Switzerland? Or can we be on a train, on the Orient Express?" Or they would ask questions that would qualify where they could be. [When you find people who ask] questions like that, that [indicates the person is a] critical thinker, a person who is always looking for a better solution, who is willing to work and be in a team of an exchange of open ideas and argue strongly for their point, but be willing to see it. That's a hard thing to find, but that's the ideal sort of person you want to have on a management team.

Hiring and Firing

With recruiters and so on you tend to go through "Well, did they go to Stanford? Did they go to Harvard? How many years have they worked?" That stuff's important, not to minimize it, but we found it's the quality of the thinking, teamwork, and exchange of ideas that are the elements that set extraordinary teams apart from ordinary management teams.

TAKEAWAYS

⚑ The biggest issue companies have is people. And too many companies have a tendency not to get the best people, both inside and outside.

⚑ People tend to hire people like themselves, or people they're comfortable with. But that doesn't always make for the best management team.

Hiring and Firing

❧ The best management team, from day one, is one that is open and critical during a discovery phase but pulls behind a decision with 100 percent commitment.

❧ The quality of the thinking, teamwork, and exchange of ideas are the elements that set extraordinary teams apart from ordinary management teams.

Do Your Due Diligence on Prospective Employers

Colin Day

CFO, Reckitt Benckiser plc

ONE OF THE VALUABLE things I've learned over the years is not to rush to a decision in terms of perception of people or businesses. When I was first approached to join the board of easyJet, back in the year 2000, I was somewhat concerned by the prospect of what sort of business it was—its management and leadership style.

The only thing I'd previously known about this business, other than having flown easyJet a couple of times, was what I had read in the newspapers about the leader: the chairman, chief executive, and founder, Stelios [Sir Stelios Haji-Ioannou].

It was very easy to form a judgment that this was not a serious business, at the time. This business was not here to stay, and it was being run by what many people had described as a playboy entrepreneur who was in it to make a quick return.

When I was asked to join the board of easyJet as a nonexecutive director prior to the flotation on the stock market, my concern was: Were all these things actually relevant? Were these issues that would concern me in my role as a company director?

For me, the phrase "Never judge a book by its cover" is particularly relevant here because I could have easily judged that project—

Hiring and Firing

joining the board and the flotation of easy-
Jet onto the stock market—as something
other than a serious business proposition.
I was proved completely wrong, because
when I met Stelios and I started to work with
him, I soon found out that he was a very serious, focused, and detailed individual who
knew what he was doing, understood the
business, and had high integrity, standards,
and governance.

For me, the key lessons coming out of
this particular instance were, first, don't believe what you read. Second, look at the individual situation or the individual yourself
and ask them, or people like them, some
relevant questions about how they would
do things.

I try now to do that when I recruit people. I say to them, "You should do your due
diligence on me because it's very important
that you understand me and how I work. I
want you to talk to people to the left and
right of me so you have a good understand-
ing about my style. I can tell you anything I
like, and you may have a view or not, but it's

best to get views from people who have either worked directly for me, with me, or who interact with me."

I always try to give a list of people that potential recruits can draw on, because I've recognized in this incident with easyJet that perhaps people might judge me by my cover, not the content. The lesson for me was, if I've done that to somebody, are they doing that to me?

It is very easy to draw the wrong conclusion—from afar or from something you read—as opposed to engaging with that individual early on. That for me is the important point.

TAKEAWAYS

⊰ When considering a career move, keep an open mind. Forming judgments about the business or its people too quickly is likely to result in mis-perceptions.

⚏ Don't believe what you read about your prospective employer. Look instead at the individual and ask them questions about how they would do things.

⚏ If you are the one responsible for hiring, ask candidates to do due diligence. Make sure they understand you and how you work.

⚏ It is very easy to draw the wrong conclusion, as opposed to engaging with an individual early on. Remember to judge a book by its content, not its cover.

The Opera Singer

Nicola Horlick

Founder and CEO, Bramdean Asset Management LLP

I THINK TEAMWORK is essential to the smooth running of a business, and I actually think there's been quite a major change in the way people think over the last twenty years. I started working twenty years ago, and there was much more of a hierarchical approach to everything. Although I work in financial services, I spend my life analyzing businesses across every sector. I have perceived a definite change, which is that rather than these very hierarchical structures, people are moving much towards flatter structures, and teamwork is much, much more important.

I think it's very important when you are putting together a team not to fill it with people who are like you. So, for example, if we had a team of people who were all like me, it would be a disaster. It's very important, I think, to have people with differing skills.

One thing that struck me when I started at SG Warburg, which was twenty years ago, was that the people I started with were very diverse, a diverse group. There were ten people; it was half women, half men. That was extremely unusual at that point in time in the city. They were also very diverse in terms of where they came from. There were a couple of Canadians, an Indian, a couple of English people, a Danish person, a varied group of people, lots of different cultural backgrounds, lots of different educational backgrounds. It was a true meritocracy, which is very important if you're going to be a successful organization, but also it had this diversity.

So what I've sought to do in my business life is to try and emulate what I saw on that first day when I started at Warburg, which is to achieve a degree of diversity. I'm going to find the best possible person for the job, and I am completely open-minded about who that person might be.

I once was approached by an opera singer who had been at Oxford University, studied music at Oxford University, and then tried very hard for the following seven years to be an opera singer. He had had a degree of success but realized that he was never going to be an internationally renowned or acclaimed opera singer. He decided to throw it all in. He was getting married; he was looking to have children; he felt he needed to earn a more stable living. He wrote to twenty City organizations, asking if they would give him an interview. Every single one of them said no.

Hiring and Firing

I actually knew this guy's brother-in-law, who was a City lawyer. He approached me and said, "This guy's having a really hard time trying to get anything. Do you think you could help?" I said, "Well, why doesn't he come and do a couple of months with me? If it's a success, there might be some employment at the end of it. If it's not a success, then at least he's got something to put on his CV when he's writing to these City institutions." So that's what we did.

He came along and he worked for me for two months. I thought this guy was highly intelligent and would learn very fast. I said to him, "What I'm prepared to do is to employ you basically as a graduate trainee. I'm going to pay you a graduate trainee wage. But you have to understand that you're twenty-eight, and the graduate trainees are twenty-one or twenty-two. So you're going to be older than them, and bracketed with them, and put in the same boat as them. You have to understand that music is not a very good background for managing money.

Hiring and Firing

You have to take exams." He said he was prepared to accept that; he wanted the job.

He turned out to be a wonderful success. There were lots of raised eyebrows at the time. Everybody thought, "What is she doing, employing an opera singer to try and be a fund manager?" In the end they all rather agreed with me and thought he was excellent. It is very important, I think, to make sure that there are people who have different strengths and abilities, different backgrounds, and different aptitudes.

Sometimes you get situations where a person in a team might be particularly good at something and might become very critical of another person who's not quite so good at that particular thing. And then it's very important to point out to [the second person] that while they may be not particularly good at that aspect of their job, they're brilliant at some other aspect of their job. And that's why they're there.

Some tension is essential in a team. I'm not asking these people to go out every night together, and have dinner together, and have Sunday lunch together. I want them to work as a team, and therefore, you do need a bit of tension there in order to make that work. But be very, very careful not to let that get out of control, because politics, in any organization, can be a disaster and can destroy an organization.

If you're going to have a team-based approach, you cannot reward people on their individual performance alone. You have to have a big element that is related to the performance of the team as a whole, and you have to keep ramming home that message and saying, "You will be rewarded for your contribution to this team." As long as you keep doing that, people get that message, and they then will try very hard to make sure that they do contribute.

There must be some sort of personal element involved as well in terms of rewarding, because some people are more talented than others. You can't, however egalitarian you are in your approach, reward everybody equally, because that's not really fair on the person who is particularly talented.

I think what's happened is quite a fundamental change in the way that people work. I really, truly believe that if you take a group of highly intelligent people and put them together with a common aim and clear leadership, they're going to achieve an awful lot more than a disparate group of people.

TAKEAWAYS

- ⊨ Teamwork is essential to the smooth running of a business, especially in businesses that have a flatter structure instead of a more traditional, hierarchical structure.

- ⊨ When putting together a team, avoid hiring clones of yourself. Hire people who have different strengths and abilities, backgrounds, and aptitudes.

⊨ While some tension in a team is essential, be very careful not to let it get out of control. Politics can destroy any organization.

⊨ When you put together a group of highly intelligent people with a common aim and clear leadership, they will achieve far more than a disparate group of people.

Recruit Talent, Not Experience

Sir Donald Cruickshank

Former Chairman, London Stock Exchange plc

YOU'RE SO OFTEN, as an interviewer, or part of a panel interviewing people, faced with an array of candidates who have been selected through a process that has valued very highly their experience, as their previous experience palpably and observably equipped them to play this role that we are now advertising or trying to fill. But I find myself sitting there thinking, "God, these are dull." Yes, they could all do the job, and maybe two of them are above the line, but by recruiting this person, are we really raising the potential and the energy of the organization to tackle the big issues it has to tackle?

Then I found myself as director general of Oftel, and I inherited a weak team of civil servants who had been, by and large, assigned from the Department of Trade and Industry (DTI) to work at Oftel. Now, guess the quality of the talent that had been assigned by one organization to serve another, particularly since the Department of Trade and Industry saw Oftel as a subsidiary.

We started advertising instead of accepting assignments from the DTI. And because it was coming through a civil-service HR process, we were still getting "This person's had all the relevant experience of the right person." And I thought, "Now look, look, look. There are some people here who have applied who may not have the seniority or direct experience, but they just seem remarkably talented people. Let's at least recruit some on the basis of their potential and take a risk." I was able to enforce that, and it turned out to be absolutely the case. Indeed, maybe a year to eighteen months later, the whole of the senior management team at Oftel, which was the team that was going to do all the basic thinking and driving forward, had come from shifting the criteria to potential and talent, and away from experience.

That's something that I've applied ever since. The chief executive of the London Stock Exchange, Clara Furse, is an example of that. I had to recruit a chief executive. The pressure was to recruit someone who was experienced in the equities market, who had relevant experience being a chief executive of a public corporation, and so on. But I spied in Clara someone who wasn't from the equities market; she had spent all her life in derivatives, bonds, and commodities; she hadn't really had chief executive experience in a public corporation. And now she has blossomed, and that organization is far better led than it's ever been.

Hiring and Firing

One of the interesting, and at first unacknowledged, outcomes of this process is that you end up with many more women, many more minorities, many more younger people. And I've found that particularly the recruitment of talented women does so much for an organization—a lovely secondary benefit of "Recruit talent and potential, and downplay experience."

TAKEAWAYS

⚏ Avoid hiring people simply because they can do what the job requires.

⚏ Always ask the question, "In recruiting this person, are we really raising the potential and the energy of the organization to tackle the big issues?"

Hiring and Firing

- ⚐ Take a risk. Don't dismiss people because they lack seniority or direct experience. Many of these people are remarkably talented.

- ⚐ Recruit talent and potential. Down-play experience.

Populate Your Inner Circle with Experts

Laura Tyson

Former Dean, London Business School

THIS IS A LESSON about the people you bring in to work with you, and the importance of getting the very best people you can. Even if in some cases they have such strong reputations that you might think they're going to compete with you for repu-

tational benefit, in fact, they're going to
help you.

Perhaps because I view life as one long
learning process, I have always believed that
the way you learn is by having really smart
people around you. If they're smarter than
you, that's even better.

I was brought in to chair a council of economic advisers. Normally, the distinction
between the chair and the two members is
a pretty important one. So the chairman—
the head—is usually, by general reputation,
considered to be quite a significant leader
relative to the two members.

My view was to try to bring in members
who were at the absolute top of their profes-
sion. Indeed, the two members I brought in
were considered to be top-notch in their
fields. I felt that to have such people around
me would allow me to do my job better and
would also allow the institution to achieve its
mission better. I didn't draw any distinction
hierarchically between myself and them, but
one of these individuals has gone on to win
the Nobel Prize in economics, while another

became the vice chairman of the Federal Reserve, so I think I chose pretty well.

I brought these people into every room with me; they were not just my deputies, they were my coequals. I created that atmosphere. The benefits were twofold. First, I received huge reputational benefits for running the council like that, for being able to attract such talent, and for treating such talent without any sense of hierarchy at all. Second, the organization that I led—and the advice we gave to the president—was as good as it could possibly be because I had brought in this level of expertise.

I think it's very important for people at the head of organizations not to be afraid of having the smartest people in the room—and, indeed, people who are smarter than they are. This really has to do with recognizing what your competence is and what you need around you. But when you need individuals of that level of accomplishment, you also have to think about ways to engage them. To my mind, in many cases that means having no hierarchy at all. Essentially, it's a team of equals.

TAKEAWAYS

- ⚑ Get the very best people you can. Although you might think they will compete with you, they will actually be able to help you.

- ⚑ Surround yourself with smart people— or better still, with people who are smarter than you. Having such people on your team helps both you and the organization perform at higher levels.

- ⚑ Engage top talent by treating them as if there were no organizational hierarchy. Doing so will help you attract more top talent.

The Long-Range View over Short-Term Expediency

Gerry Roche

Senior Chairman, Heidrick & Struggles International, Inc.

THE MOST IMPORTANT perspective to have in life is the long-range view over short-term expediency. That's at the core of our business and every business. It's at the core of your relationships with each other;

with your wife, friends, and family; and at the core of your relationship with whatever God you might worship.

Roberto Goizueta, the former chairman and CEO of Coca-Cola, once asked me if I was interested in a search to find a CFO for Coke. My insides were going crazy because I knew that he had a very good guy, who was the CFO of Coca-Cola Europe.

I said, "Roberto, before you commission this search—do you know your CFO in Europe?" He replied, "I just got this job, so no, I've never met him. I don't even know his name. Who is he?" I told him his CFO of Europe was a guy named Doug Ivester.

I got a call two weeks later from Roberto, and he said, "Gerry, I can't thank you enough. I met with this man; he's my answer. Do I owe you a fee?" And I said, "No, not for two weeks' work, and not for that. But there will be a time, Roberto, when we would like to do more work for Coke. But God bless you, and I'm happy." Doug Ivester turned out to be a first-rate CFO, so much so that he became the president of Coke.

Hiring and Firing

Eight years after that I got a call from Roberto Goizueta. He said, "Hey, Gerry, I am the chairman of the search committee for Kodak. They told me that I should have a beauty contest and take a look at a couple of firms. But I remember you and your integrity and honesty from ten years ago, and I appreciate the favor you did me with Douglas. If you are willing to do this search, you've got it. Come on down to Atlanta, and we'll talk about it and write up the specs." Bing-bang, no competition, no shoot-out. We got the search for the chairman and CEO of Kodak.

Eight years is the long-range view. I think everything comes down to the long-range view.

When I finished with Nike we had what I thought was a great candidate a year ago. We presented him to Phil Knight, the board, and the lead director. Everybody liked him a lot; his personality and his experience were fine. I personally wound up doing the references on this fellow. They weren't bad; they just weren't dead-on. I can always sense that, instead of "Oh, he's tremendous; you'd be lucky to get him; I don't think you'll ever get him." I know how to take references, and I know the difference between the pulse of a great one and one that's modulating and waffling. His references were modulating and waffling just enough to give me angst and heartburn.

I was sighing and saying to myself, "Dear God, I've been doing this search for six months. It could be over. But I have to tell Phil what I found out, and I have to be honest about my doubts about this person."

I told Phil Knight, and we wound up doing more references on [this candidate] and flushing him. I told Nike, "It would have been easy for me to say, 'Hey, he's all right.' But I'm saying, 'Hey, I want to feel Knight's respect twenty years from now. Phil Knight has a great company; he deserves to have a great CEO. He doesn't deserve to have one who has yellow flags.'"

I filled the CEO position with a guy named Bill Perez, who was the chairman and CEO of SC Johnson. Phil is happier now with Bill than he was with the other guy, by far. He says, "We dodged a bullet." The yellow flags about that other fellow have since become red.

The long-range view over short-term expediency wins every time. Not immediately— sometimes it's painful and it costs. But if you have faith in the future, you have the long-range view.

TAKEAWAYS

- At the core of every business is the ability to take the long-term view over short-term expediency.

- When recruiting, take your time. Get the best possible person for the job, not someone who is just "all right."

Hiring and Firing

⤝ Follow up on references, and listen to your instincts. If it doesn't feel right, find out more about the candidate. Great companies deserve nothing less than great people.

⤝ Having faith in the future means you have the long-range view, and the long-range view wins every time.

Focus on Retaining Talent, Not Hiring

Jody Thompson
and Cali Ressler

*Cofounders, CultureRx (a subsidiary
of Best Buy Co, Inc.)*

Hiring and Firing

JODY THOMPSON: Companies today are looking to figure out how to hire the right talent. In our experience we've found that if you shift your focus to retaining the talent that you have, and look at people who potentially aren't doing the work and let them go work somewhere else, you're actually creating an environment where you'll [retain] people instead of figuring out how to get them back once they've left.

When we talk about retaining people and creating the right kind of work environment, one of the things companies are going to tackle in the future is, what do we do with those crazy Gen Y-ers? That next generation, that completely untethered generation of people who are not connected to anything but their device, who are connected all over the world with their device, who have Facebook and all sorts of ways to collaborate and communicate. Then what we do is, we bring them into an environment that's completely tethered: desktop computer, a cube, meeting face-to-face with people all the time, and a manager who's managing by walking around.

Creating an environment to stick the talent that's coming is what's going to be important in the future.

I'm going to paint the picture of a Gen Y person in a tethered, traditional organization.

On Sunday night I am completely dreading the week ahead of me. I know it's coming; it starts at eight o'clock Monday morning. All week I have no control over my time or what I do, because now the company has control over that. So I get up in the morning, I'm rushing around, and I have to quickly get out in rush-hour traffic because if I'm not in my cube at eight o'clock, then I get that look: "Gee, bankers' hours again today. I was here; why weren't you here?"

So I do some work. I'm in my cube, and now I get interrupted. I try to get something done, and I get interrupted again. All day long I'm struggling to do my work. And I'm also thinking about all the other things I have to do in my life, so I surf the Internet for a while and my boss walks by. I quickly, you know, put the monitor to a different direction so they don't see it. And all day long I'm struggling, struggling, struggling because I don't have any control over my time.

Cali Ressler: That was Mark the first three weeks that he worked in the company, before he was in a results-only work environment. Here's what he looks like now: Mark is someone who has complete control over how he spends his time every single day. Sometimes he decides, "I'm going to work really hard for two weeks and then have the next two weeks where I am traveling the country, following my favorite rock band." Sometimes Mark is someone who sleeps in until eleven o'clock on a Tuesday before he calls in for a meeting, then does some grocery shopping and comes back and does some e-mails. Mark has told us he does not own an alarm clock anymore. In corporate

Hiring and Firing

America you don't hear that very often: He doesn't have an alarm clock; he lets the sun wake him up.

He is someone who can do his work while he's watching ESPN, watching his favorite game. He goes to the mountains to do some hiking, and we know that for him that is a place that gives him the spark to do his work. And today he is someone who can find that spark wherever he needs to find it, whenever he needs to find it, and that's what's made this kind of environment priceless for him.

Jody Thompson: Here's the paradigm shift for managers. If I have an employee who's sitting in a tent on a mountain, does that look like work? If my employee is sitting in a coffee shop, does that look like work? If my employee is sitting at the beach, does that look like work? So what we're shifting in a manager's mind is, what looks like work might not really be work.

If you think about your employee sitting in their cube all day, you have a false sense that they're working. You think that they're working because it looks like work—they're in the office building; they're in the cube; they have a computer in front of them; they're talking to the people around them. That looks like work. And as a manager I feel uncomfortable if I allow my people to work in other places, because I wonder if I'm not getting the hours out of them; I wonder if they're not working.

But managers in a results-only work environment look at results only—not where people are working, not what time they're working, but that they're getting the work done. That's the real shift for managers: I don't own your time anymore; I own making clear your goals and expectations.

Cali Ressler: And Mark's manager is extremely clear about goals and expectations, and Mark understands those, which is why Mark's productivity has now increased four times since he migrated to a results-only work environment.

He would never go to another company. We've asked him, "How much would a

company have to pay him to leave Best Buy?"
And he says to us, "They couldn't pay me
enough money. I will never leave this. Why
would I leave this job that I have that allows
me to live exactly how I've always wanted
to live?"

Jody Thompson: Companies today are focused on hiring the right talent. What companies should be looking at is creating an
environment that sticks the talent that they
have. They'll spend less time hiring and
more time getting work done.

TAKEAWAYS

⚐ Today's companies too often spend
   their time trying to hire the right talent. Instead, they should shift their
   focus toward retaining existing talent.

Hiring and Firing

⚜ Creating an environment that will "stick," or retain, the talent that's coming in—Generation Y—is what will be important in the future. That means creating a results-only work environment.

⚜ This is a paradigm shift for many managers. They must recognize that what traditionally looked like work might not actually be work.

⚜ In results-based work environments, productivity often increases, allowing managers to spend less time hiring and more time getting work done.

Hire People
with Integrity

Sir Mark Weinberg

Cofounder and President, St. James's Place Capital

THE KEY TO a successful company is always good people—good people all the way up, but particularly, good people in top management. And that means the ability to work together, the ability to grow in their jobs, and so on. But there's also another element that isn't so fully recognized, and that's integrity. Now, I've once or twice in my career had the experience of dealing with people whose ethics are not the ethics that I would like. And ultimately, it comes back and bites you.

To give you an example of this, I was involved in forming a company. And one of the key people, whom I'd worked with on a previous occasion but somewhat remotely, was a party to forming the new company. We sat down and agreed to the terms on which we would work together, and then, after we'd shaken hands, this one person suddenly came along and he said, "My terms for staying with this enterprise"—and he was very closely linked in by then—"is that I want an extra hundred thousand pounds as a bonus at the end of year one." We all said, "But you never mentioned that before, and we all agreed what the fair terms are." And he said, "Those are my terms; otherwise, I'm not going ahead." We were dependent on him, so we did go ahead with him.

I subsequently said to him, "Why did you do that? Because it doesn't create a very good impression." He said that his father had been a union official, and he'd taught him when he was very young that when you're in negotiations with somebody, a boss or something or other, that after you've reached agreement after a long, hard negotiation, you should always come back and ask for one more thing, because the person will never refuse, because you've gone to all this trouble. They don't want to unwind the whole thing. And he'd successfully done that.

I and my other colleagues felt uneasy about it, and we just thought, "Well, that's a pretty tough way to run life, but maybe he'll be tough with our competitors. Maybe it's not so bad to have a person like that."

We then subsequently got involved in a dispute with somebody else, and again we'd settled the dispute. And when we'd settled the dispute, he suddenly came along afterwards and insisted on something else. Once again, I nearly had a heart attack because it was going to break up a very important negotiation. Once again, he sort of smiled and said this was his father's lesson.

Hiring and Firing

Three or four years later we got into a problem where we were on opposite sides as to what we would do with a company, and he then—and I don't want to get into details of it now; it's not relevant—behaved in a way that put his own interests completely ahead of the interests of everybody else in the company, and we eventually had to part company because we had to face up to him. But I actually realized then the price of ignoring the risks of taking someone on who has a different ethical front. Integrity is important. You may not notice at the time; you might even find that, OK, it's good to have a tough guy with you. But I think in the end, integrity is something that will come back and bite you if you ignore it.

I think it's very important for the key people in the company to have their own ethical standards, and to agree to them amongst themselves, and to stick to them. I think you regret it if you don't. The more difficult question is how you decide whether somebody on your team, perhaps a new

Hiring and Firing

person who's coming in, has that integrity. And I'm afraid there's no easy answer to that. In fact, that's part of a general problem when you're interviewing somebody new for a job—how do you decide they are good?

I think one of the answers to both the general question and the specific one on ethics is that when you're talking to people about joining the company, the employer tends to talk too much. The only way you're going to find out about people is by asking a few questions, keeping your mouth closed, and getting them to talk. And the more you can get them to talk, the more you'll learn about whether they're likely to be good at their jobs and also whether they're likely to have integrity.

TAKEAWAYS

⚔ The key to a successful company is always good people, particularly good people in top management. Integrity is an important part of this.

⚔ A company that retains employees whose ethics are either questionable or at odds with its current leaders will eventually pay a price.

⚔ One way to determine whether people possess high ethical standards is to ask them questions and keep your mouth closed. The more they talk, the more you'll learn.

⚔ If you ignore it, integrity is something that will come back and bite you.

———◆◆◆———

Remove People Sooner Rather Than Later

Erroll Davis Jr.

Former Chairman, President and CEO,
Alliant Energy Corp.

———◆◆◆———

I BELONG TO a presidents' group, and we sometimes ask ourselves, "Have you done anything you regret? Is there a decision that you would like to make over again?"

Hiring and Firing

The interesting part of all of these discussions with my peers, even with those who have been through what you see as very cataclysmic business cycles, is that very few of them talk about making different strategy decisions. They talk about people decisions: that they should have taken people out of jobs sooner who were not performing and meeting expectations. Because of a sense of compassion for the individual, they let the situation get out of hand. In retrospect, their compassion for the company and the investor should have outweighed their compassion for the individual.

I find that as I look back on my career, I ask myself if there are things that I should have done differently. In every instance that I think about, it comes down to taking someone out of a job sooner rather than later.

I think that we need to impress upon individuals that being taken out of a job is not a moral flaw or a character indictment. It's merely recognition that you are not meeting our expectations. You are not doing what we

Hiring and Firing

want you to do in this job, and the risk to other employees of leaving you in there is too high. We cannot tell employees, "You are the most important part of the company" and then put bad supervision in front of them. If we have bad supervisors, take them out of the job immediately. You don't have to fire them; you can retrain them. If they're not capable of being supervisors, are they capable of being good single contributors? Again, I think it's important to have the discipline and the edge to move quickly.

I believe that it is not incompatible to be both tough and compassionate; it's the same discussion between mercy and justice. We must have justice, order, and structure, and we hope that justice will be delivered with compassion and tempered with mercy. I believe that's the way you have to run your business: you have to have the order and the structure first. You have to do the things that are right for your shareowners, your customers, and for the general employee group, even if it means that you have to inflict pain. People in our positions have to inflict pain periodically.

I've also found over time that people who are not performing know that they're not performing. Time and time again I've found that people are relieved to be taken out of situations where they don't see a way to be successful in those jobs. The last thing it should be is a surprise to them. If it's a surprise to them, then you haven't done your job. You haven't communicated your expectations; you haven't communicated how they're meeting those expectations; you haven't communicated the shortfalls or ramifications to them. [Firing an employee] should be easier than it is if we do our job.

It's the hardest thing to be judgmental, because people don't want to be. But if I take a room full of ten highly motivated, highly educated people and say to them, "I'm going to rate you all intellectually. Raise your hand if you believe you're below average," no one raises their hands. But from a statistical perspective, half of them have to be, no matter how smart the group is.

People just don't like to be judgmental, but when you're put in positions of authority, you have to be.

TAKEAWAYS

⚜ Regrets and mistakes occur more frequently in people decisions than in strategy decisions.

⚜ When decisions are based purely on compassion for the individual, it can be detrimental to an organization's success. Maintain focus on what's best for the company and its investors.

⚜ Being taken out of a job is not a moral flaw or a character indictment; it's merely recognition that a person is not performing well in a given position.

⚞ Once you recognize that a person is not performing, move quickly. Do what's right for the company, even if it results in short-term pain for the individual.

How to Let People Go

John Roberts

Former CEO, United Utilities

IF YOU HAVE SOMEONE who is not
performing properly, in my experience
the best way to approach it is to first have a
proper system of appraisal that ensures that,
on a regular basis, you sit down with people
and talk to them about their performance.

If their performance is not at the level
that you want it to be, be open about that.

Hiring and Firing

Explain to [the person] that they have deficiencies, that there are shortcomings. Get them to recognize that, because not everybody recognizes that they're not doing things as well as they could. Everybody thinks they're doing a great job.

The second thing is to agree with them how you're going to try and rectify those deficiencies. Is it training? Is it more help? Is it maybe a change of job?

If you have that properly documented, it's a benchmark that you have—an agreed-upon benchmark. Then, if you find that the person, despite all your best endeavors, is not improving, if you then have to terminate them, the first thing is, you have to do it face-to-face. The second thing is, if you've built up an agreed-upon set of [criteria] that they're not performing, you can say, "Look, we had this conversation at such and such a time, so many weeks before. We agreed that you would do this, and your performance had to improve; it hasn't."

And if you demonstrate that there's a logical process behind it, that it's not just an

Hiring and Firing

emotional reaction—I don't like you; you're out—but instead "Look, here is a logical process, and you can see where it's leading. The logical conclusion is you don't fit with the organization, you don't deliver the performance we want—therefore, you're going." It makes the most sense and gives you the most logical platform by which to do it. Not everybody will respond to that logic. People can get quite emotional. But from my experience, [this process] puts you in a very secure position.

Actually firing someone, sitting down face-to-face opposite someone and saying, "You are no longer going to work for us" is a very difficult situation, probably the most fraught things that an individual manager has to do. You have to think very carefully through each case on an individual basis. From your knowledge of the individual, what kind of reaction are you likely to get? Is this a situation in which the evidence that you want to bring into play is not absolutely clear-cut—where, for example, there aren't obvious failings of gross misconduct or whatever; where it's more just a series of events, a body of evidence [that] slowly accumulates; where you reach the point where you know you can't go any further? Then I think one needs to think about, what is the reaction going to be? And is there a possibility this person's going to try and sue the business for unfair dismissal, take some kind of action in those directions? Are they going to get angry? Is it going to get very fraught? Are there going to be accusations flying around?

Quite often, in those cases, it's very helpful just to write down all the things that you think they're likely to bring up, the points that they're likely to make. Think about what your answer is going to be to each of those points. Why are you doing this? What are the kinds of objections that they are likely to bring up? What's going to be your response to that?

If you're at all concerned about that person leaving that interview with a different view of what was said than the one that you have, and perhaps taking you or the business to court, taking further action, then my strong advice would be to have a reliable witness. Normally that's someone like the head of human relations or head of industrial relations, somebody who is reasonably dispassionate but reliable and senior, and whom you feel comfortable with, whom you don't mind having in the room at the same time to go through what is normally—let's face it—a fairly uncomfortable process. Have a witness—who doesn't have to say anything, but at least they can be there so that after the event you have an independent witness of what happened.

The other thing I would say is, once you've gone through the process, the termination, done the interview, then the sensible thing is to write up a note of what you think was said, what was agreed, and what was discussed, and make sure that your witness sees it and agrees with it. You need a proper record of what happened, because after the event, the person who was dismissed will have a lot of emotional turmoil; their recollection of the events will be highly biased, and understandably, highly colored. And they'll probably go away with quite a different view of the world and what went on than the one that you think went on. You want to be absolutely clear that you have it on the record.

Once you've dealt with it, then you need to move on as quickly as you can, and that person exits the organization. You do all you can to help them if you think that's appropriate, but you have to make the decision positively.

TAKEAWAYS

🖎 Having a formal appraisal system is key when addressing the performance issues of employees because it gives managers an on-going opportunity to talk with employees about any performance shortcomings.

Hiring and Firing

🙼 When firing an employee becomes necessary, managers must consider the person involved and prepare for any reactions that individual might have.

🙼 If there is a fear that the terminated individual might pursue legal action, have a witness present during the termination meeting and make a formal record of the meeting's events.

🙼 Afterward, move on as quickly as possible.

—•◀◆▶•—

Don't Deliver
Bad News Badly

—•◀◆▶•—

Paul Anderson

Chairman, Spectra Energy Corp.

EARLY ON IN MY CAREER, I had probably my most embarrassing lesson, which was:
Don't try to sugarcoat bad news. It happened
the first time that I was put in a position
where I had to fire someone. I think for all
people the first time you have to fire someone—in fact, any time you have to fire
someone—you're basically uncomfortable.

Hiring and Firing

It's not pleasant news, it's a difficult situation, and so you try to figure out the easiest way to get the story out without appearing to be a bad guy.

I gathered my thoughts and went down to the HR department, and I said, "I'm going to be firing George this afternoon, and you might expect to see his face at your door. I'll send him down to figure out his options with regard to termination payments and so on and so forth." I felt I was pretty well prepared.

I called George in that afternoon, and I said, "George, things just aren't working out. We have some problems here." I explained why he wasn't contributing to the organization. I said, "I'm sorry to tell you this, but you're just going to have to look for another job. I think the next step is for you to go down and talk to the folks in Personnel, and then you can figure out what your options are from there."

I thought, "Well, that wasn't too bad; George didn't seem particularly upset." He was concerned—he was sorry it wasn't working out—but he certainly didn't seem as upset as I would have been if somebody had just fired me.

The next morning I came in—and so did George. He was sitting there at the desk just as if nothing had happened. I went over and said, "George, why are you here?" He replied, "I'm here working on this project." I asked, "Didn't you understand our discussion yesterday?" He answered, "Yes, I did. I understand that I'm not working out in this position and that I should go down to Personnel and talk about what other options there are within the company for me to find another job."

I thought about it and realized that was probably not an unfair interpretation of what I said, because I wasn't that straight-forward. I didn't say, "You need to find another job outside this company; you're fired." His state of mind was such that he didn't want to hear that.

Ultimately, I had to replay the conversation to him, explain to him that he was indeed fired, take him to Personnel, and

complete the task. It was much more unpleasant to have two conversations instead of
getting it out in the first one.

But it taught me—and I learned more and
more the higher up I got in the organization—that if you think you're doing people
favors by sugarcoating news, or if you think
you're making your life easier by being
somewhat oblique in the way you deliver bad
news, you're kidding yourself.

There's no substitute for straightforward,
between-the-eyes truth. If you're at all ob-
scure about what you're telling them, they
will hear what they want to hear, and they're
predisposed, either positively or negatively,
toward news. They're going to hear what they
want to hear if you aren't straightforward.

This actually goes for good news as well
as bad. In many cases, I've delivered what I
thought was good news—for instance, "We're
going to have retention agreements with
everybody during this pending merger so
that you can rest easy." Instead, they hear,
"There's going to be massive layoffs, but

they're going to give us retention agreements until they lay us off."

So you really have to think through what the message is that you're sending, be absolutely straightforward, and then deliver that message. The only thing worse than delivering bad news is delivering it badly.

TAKEAWAYS

⚔ Don't try to "sugarcoat" bad news, particularly when the bad news results in someone being fired.

⚔ When news is not delivered in a clear manner, there is room for misinterpretation of the message. In these cases, people will hear what they want to hear.

Hiring and Firing

- There's no substitute for straightforward, between-the-eyes truth—a lesson that holds true for good news as well.

- The only thing worse than delivering bad news is delivering it badly.

Letting People Go

Lord Sharman

Chairman, Aegis Group plc

FIRST AND FOREMOST, the issue of reductions in head count is one that I have a personal philosophy about: that when you need to make those decisions, you need to make them quickly. You shouldn't hang over them, because people are bright. They're intelligent; they know what's going on; they can see that the sales aren't coming in or whatever. The longer you hang on, the more disruptive and the more unpleasant it becomes for the individuals involved.

So you make the decision quickly, and then you implement it kindly. And what that means is helping people move out of the organization. [At KPMG, the first time I had to do this, we had quite a big redundancy program—I think it was about 400 people . . . early nineties.] We set up an in-house employment agency. We tried to select the individuals on a very open—it did not always work—but a very open, well-understood basis that was based on the individuals' performance and where they were.

Sometimes it's just the fact that you're in a certain unit, and you decide to close the unit. That's hard, but you try and redeploy people. Occasionally, not too often, then you have to let the senior people go for performance reasons. I saw one the other day. The words [he] used were, "When you fired me, it was the best thing that had ever happened to me." He said he'd become so stuck in a rut and wasn't performing well, wasn't happy, but he felt he didn't really want to take the initiative himself.

There is life outside the organization you're part of. When I go back and talk to the people at KPMG from time to time, I always start off by saying, "I'm pleased to tell you there is life outside KPMG; I'm the living manifestation of it." But it is a traumatic time for people. You have to understand that; you have to see it from their point of view. The tendency is to try and be a bit like "Keep it away from me; I don't want to deal with this because it's difficult." And it is a difficult process, probably the most difficult thing you have to do in your career.

TAKEAWAYS

⊲ When faced with the issue of having to reduce head count—whether it's based on budget or on performance—make decisions quickly.

- People are smart, and they'll figure out what's going on. The longer the situation lingers, the more disruptive and unpleasant it becomes.

- After making the decision to let people go, be compassionate and provide as much support as possible.

- Recognize that letting someone go is probably the most difficult thing you'll do as a manager.

Be Tough but Compassionate

Peter Ellwood

Group Chairman, Imperial Chemical Industries

A MANAGER NEEDS TO BE tough but, at the same time, compassionate. I remember making a mistake by fudging an issue when I was chief executive of the TSB banking group in the nineties. I had to deal with a guy who was a fellow board member, who was very senior. He'd worked for the company for thirty years and given it a really good shot and was doing OK, but I wanted somebody who was doing brilliantly. He wasn't really performing; his numbers weren't coming through. When I used to see him on a regular basis, he used to ask me questions and ask me to make decisions that, frankly, he should have been making. I would then ask him about his business, and he wouldn't really know the answers as well as he should have.

In fact, I knew more about his business than he did, and that's when I started to get really worried. I decided to try and offer him a lesser job. It was still quite an important job, but he prevaricated for about a month or so.

I said, "Hey, we need to know whether you're going to take this job or not." I had allowed him to make the organization somewhat carcinogenic because clearly he was not a happy bunny. In the end, I got him in one evening and I said, "Look, this is not going to work. You are going to have to go. Why don't we say the story is that you have elected to go and you want to do lots of different things?"

So I got tough, and he went compassionately and was able to spin the story that it was of his own volition. Since then I have not given people that luxury. If I've thought "they have to go," then they've gone and they've gone quickly.

Don't fudge issues; don't assume that they might go away. If you know in your heart—and it is an emotional as well as a mental thing—that somebody is not right for the job, that somebody else could do their job more effectively and be world-class, then you have to act. You owe it to yourself, your team, and ultimately your shareholders.

My direct reports come to see me on a monthly basis for a fairly formal session, and they talk about their people. In fact, if they don't talk about how their people have been getting on over the previous four weeks, I will always raise the issue, because the most important thing any manager does is manage other people.

Hiring and Firing

So when a manager tells me, "We're thinking about Bert. He's not doing terribly well, but I think he'll be all right," I say, "Well, you told me that Bert wasn't doing terribly well two months ago. How long are you going to give him?" And he says, "Well, I'm working on him." I suggest, "Let's decide that if he's not doing well in, say, two months from now, he's out."

So I help managers to think about crystallizing their own thoughts about their people. One of the most important things a manager has to do is to live in the real world and not pretend that things will all be right. If he knows that he has to take action, a good manager always grasps the nettle, but he does it with sensitivity and compassion.

TAKEAWAYS

- ⚑ Managers need to be tough but, at the same time, compassionate.

- ⚑ When you know that a person is not right for the job, act quickly. You owe it to yourself, your team, and your shareholders.

- ⚑ The most important thing you will do as a manager is manage other people. Find out how your employees are doing and, if necessary, set a timeline to help them improve.

- ⚑ If improvement is not seen, take the steps necessary to remove the person from the position. But do so with sensitivity.

⊰ ABOUT THE ⊱
CONTRIBUTORS

Paul Anderson is chairman of Spectra Energy
Corp., a natural-gas company.

Mr. Anderson started his career at Ford Motor
Co., holding various positions in marketing, product engineering, finance, and manufacturing from
1969 to 1972. He was planning manager from 1972
until 1977, when he joined PanEnergy Corp.

Over the ensuing years Mr. Anderson served in
various leadership roles within the company, cul-
minating in his becoming its chairman, president,
and CEO. When PanEnergy merged with Duke
Power Co. in 1997, he became president and chief
operating officer of Duke Energy Corp. for a year,
following his key leadership role in the merger.

He then moved to BHP Ltd. in 1998, where he
was managing director and CEO until 2001, when
the company merged with Billiton plc. He became
managing director and CEO of BHP Billiton Ltd.
(the Australian-listed company) and BHP Billiton
plc (the U.K.-listed company) until his retirement
in July 2002.

Mr. Anderson returned to Duke Energy as its
chairman and CEO in November 2003. He then
became chairman of Spectra Energy in 2007 when

Duke Energy's natural-gas business was spun off into this new company.

He is also a director of Qantas Airways Ltd. and BHP Billiton.

Sir Donald Cruickshank is the former chairman of London Stock Exchange plc. Currently, he is a director of Qualcomm Inc.

Sir Donald was a consultant at McKinsey & Co. before joining Times Newspapers as commercial director, then moving to the role of managing director of the information and entertainment division of Pearson plc. In 1984 he became managing director of Virgin Group plc, where he spent the next five years.

He was chief executive of the National Health Service in Scotland from 1989 to 1993, then became director general of the U.K.'s Office of Telecommunications (Oftel), a position he held from 1993 to 1998. He spent three years as chairman of Action 2000, the U.K. government's millennium bug campaign.

Sir Donald was appointed by then chancellor, Gordon Brown, to be chairman of the Government's review of the UK banking sector in 1998. His report was published in March 2000.

He became chairman of the London Stock Exchange in May 2000, a position from which he stepped down in July 2003. He became a director of Qualcomm in 2005. Until recently, he was also chairman of the media group SMG plc.

About the Contributors

Erroll Davis Jr. is the former chairman of Alliant Energy Corp. Currently, he is the chancellor of the University System of Georgia.

Mr. Davis has worked in the energy industry for over 25 years. He joined Wisconsin Power and Light Co. in 1978, became CEO ten years later, and also served as president until 1998.

Following the merger in 1998, Mr. Davis became president and CEO of Alliant Energy. He stayed in the role of CEO until June 2005 and remained chairman of the company until 2006, when he stepped down.

Mr. Davis also served as CEO of Alliant Energy Resources, Inc. and Iowa Power and Light Co. (or their predecessor companies) following the merger.

In February 2006 he took office as chancellor of the University System of Georgia. Mr. Davis is on the boards of BP plc, Union Pacific Corp., and the Edison Electric Institute.

Colin Day is chief financial officer and a director of Reckitt Benckiser plc, a leading provider of cleaning and health and personal products.

Mr. Day started his career in 1973 as a trainee accountant at Eastman Kodak Co. A year later he joined British Gas plc, where he worked as an internal audit, management, and project accountant for five years.

In 1980 he moved to De La Rue Group plc, where he spent eight years in various financial and accounting roles within the group and its Crosfield

Electronics Ltd. subsidiary. By the end of his tenure there, he had risen to group financial controller.

In 1988 he joined ABB Group as group finance director of ABB Kent plc, moving up to become group finance director of ABB Instrumentation Ltd. In 1995 he became group finance director at Aegis Group plc, a position he held until 2000.

Mr. Day has subsequently been group chief financial officer and a director of Reckitt Benckiser for five years. He has also held the positions of director of easyJet and Bell Group plc. He became a director of WPP Group plc in 2005.

Peter Ellwood is the group chairman of Imperial Chemical Industries plc (ICI), a position he has held since January 2004.

Mr. Ellwood began his career at Barclays Bank plc in 1961 and rose to become CEO of Barclaycard from 1985 until 1989. During this time he was also a director of the board of Visa European Union. He was chairman of Visa International from 1994 to 1999.

He joined TSB Bank plc as CEO of Retail Banking in 1989 and became group CEO in 1992. Following the merger with Lloyds Bank Group in 1995, Mr. Ellwood became deputy group CEO of Lloyds TSB Group plc and then group CEO.

Mr. Ellwood became deputy chairman of ICI, one of the world's largest producers of specialty products and paints, in June 2003 and now holds the position of chairman, which he has held since January 2004.

About the Contributors

In 2001, he was made a Commander of the British Empire for services to banking. He was also chairman of The Work Foundation and is chairman of the Race Equality and Diversity Task Force of the Institute for Public Policy Research. Mr. Ellwood is a fellow of the Chartered Institute of Bankers. Since September 2005 he has been a director of First Data Corp.

Sir Richard Evans is the chairman of United Utilities plc, a position he has held since 2001.

Sir Richard started his career at the UK Ministry of Transport and Civil Aviation. He joined the British Aircraft Corp. (BAC) and was promoted to commercial director of the Warton division of British Aerospace (BAe) in 1978.

In 1981 he became deputy managing director for BAe Warton. Three years later he was made deputy managing director of the BAe military aircraft division. He was appointed to the board of BAe as marketing director and then became chairman of the British Aerospace Defense companies.

Sir Richard was appointed CEO of BAe in 1990. In 1998 he was appointed chairman of British Aerospace, and he continued to chair the company when it became BAe Systems following the merger with Marconi Electronic Systems. In July 2004, he retired from the board but continues to advise the company.

In 1997, Sir Richard joined the board of United Utilities as a director and was appointed chairman four years later.

About the Contributors

Lauren Flanagan is the cofounder and former CEO and chairman of WebWare Corp., a leader in digital asset management that was acquired by INSCI, a provider of Enterprise Content Management, in 2003. She is currently the CEO of SCIO Corp., which provides strategic advisory and specialty investment banking services.

Ms. Flanagan has more than 25 years of experience in founding and operating technology companies. Prior to forming WebWare, she cofounded four technology companies and worked as a consultant for technology leaders such as Apple Inc.; Atari, Inc.; Hewlett-Packard Co.; IBM Corp.; and Microsoft Corp. At WebWare, she helped define and lead new market categories: brand resource management (now called "marketing content management") and media asset management (now called "digital asset management"). She also served as CEO and chairman.

Ms. Flanagan is also cofounder of the Phenomenelle Angels Fund, an early-stage fund that invests in businesses that are owned or managed by women and minorities.

She is a member of the Angel Capital Association and a board observer for EraGen Biosciences, Inc., ThreeFold Sensors (IA, Inc.), and TrafficCast International, Inc.

Nicola Horlick is the founder and CEO of Bramdean Asset Management LLP, a fund management company.

About the Contributors

Ms. Horlick began her career at Mercury Asset Management plc, following a year-long graduate trainee program at SG Warburg. After eight years she moved to Morgan Grenfell Asset Management as a director of the U.K. pension fund business; she was made managing director in 1992. Over the following four years, funds under management quadrupled.

She cofounded SG Asset Management Ltd. in 1997 and was CEO of SGAM Holdings Ltd., and a senior U.K. equity fund manager, until 2003.

In 2005 Ms. Horlick founded Bramdean Asset Management.

Pamela Marrone is the founder and CEO of Marrone Organic Innovations, Inc. She is the founder and former CEO of AgraQuest, Inc.

From 1983 to 1989, Ms. Marrone led the insect biology group at Monsanto Co., developing novel solutions for controlling insects. In 1990 she left to become founding president of Entotech, Inc., a biopesticide subsidiary of Novo Nordisk A/S. After a buyout in 1995, Ms. Marrone founded Agra-Quest, a natural pest management products company. She served as its CEO, chairman, and president until April 2006.

Today, at Marrone Organic Innovations, she leads a company whose goal is to make natural, effective, safe, and environmentally friendly pest management products.

About the Contributors

Ms. Marrone serves on the boards of the Association of Applied IPM Ecologists, the National Foundation for IPM Education, and the Organic Farming Research Foundation. Since 1999 she has served on the board of Sutter Health Sacramento Sierra Region.

Cali Ressler is a cofounder of CultureRx, a wholly owned subsidiary of Best Buy Co., Inc., a specialty retailer of consumer electronics, personal computers, entertainment software, and appliances.

Ms. Ressler was a manager of Best Buy's work-life balance program when she started the ROWE (Results-Only Work Environment) experiment at a division in Minneapolis. The success of the program grew when Best Buy's "organizational guru," Jody Thompson, learned of Ms. Ressler's work and pushed to implement it as a companywide program. Together Ms. Ressler and Ms. Thompson founded CultureRx, a consulting company specializing in ROWE.

Ms. Ressler and Ms. Thompson are the coauthors of the upcoming book *Why Work Sucks and How You Can Fix It: Inside the Result-Only Revolution*. They have been featured in *BusinessWeek*, *HR Magazine*, the *New York Times*, and *TIME* magazine, and on *60 Minutes* and National Public Radio.

John Roberts is the recently retired CEO of United Utilities. Mr. Roberts graduated from Liverpool

University and joined the energy company Manweb. After working his way up in the company, he became finance director in 1984, then managing director in 1991; he was appointed chief executive a year later. He then became CEO of South Wales Electricity, being at the helm during its acquisition by Hyder, and was appointed CEO of Hyder Utilities. Mr. Roberts was appointed CEO of United Utilities in September 1999, and retired from the company in March 2006.

Mr. Roberts is a former director of Volex, a leading independent producer of electronic and fiber optic cable assemblies and electrical powercords. He also has been president of the Electricity Association and chairman of the Electricity Pension Trustees Limited.

Gerry Roche is the senior chairman of the executive search firm Heidrick & Struggles International, Inc.

In his early career Mr. Roche was an account executive for the American Broadcasting Co.; a sales manager, product manager, and marketing director for Mobil Oil Co.'s plastics subsidiary, Kordite Corp.; and a management trainee at AT&T.

Following his time at these organizations, Mr. Roche joined Heidrick & Struggles, where he has remained for more than 40 years. In 1964, he became the company's senior vice president and in 1973, eastern manager. Four years later he became executive vice president, responsible for all domestic operations. A year later Mr. Roche became president and CEO. In 1981 he moved into the chairman's role, permitting him more time to conduct high-level international search work.

In 1994, Mr. Roche cofounded Heidrick & Struggles's Office of the Chairman with John Thompson.

During his time at the firm, Mr. Roche has conducted CEO searches for companies including 3M Co., IBM Corp., Gap Inc., PricewaterhouseCoopers, and Chubb Corp.

In addition, he is on the boards of the National Mentoring Partnership (MENTOR) and the Community Anti-Drug Coalitions of America.

Lord Sharman is chairman of Aegis Group, a marketing communications company.

Lord Sharman joined Peat, Marwick, Mitchell & Co. (later KPMG International) as a manager in 1966. He worked in a number of overseas offices before being appointed a partner in the London branch in 1981.

From 1987 he was responsible for the group's national marketing, and then three years later for operations in London and the south east of England. From 1991 to 1994 he was chairman of KPMG Management Consulting worldwide. In 1994 he was appointed a senior partner.

He also served as a member of the international executive committee and on the European board. In 1997 he became chairman of KPMG International and retired from the company in September 1999.

About the Contributors

He is currently chairman of Aegis Group, a position he has held since 2000. Additionally, Lord Sharman is chairman of Aviva plc and director of Reed Elsevier and the BG Group plc. He is a member of the supervisory board of the global banking group ABN AMRO.

From 2003 to 2004 he was chairman of Securicor plc; in 2004 Lord Sharman became chairman of Group 4 Securicor plc, a leading international security services company created after Group 4 Falck's security business merged with Securicor.

Jody Thompson is a cofounder of CultureRx, a wholly owned subsidiary of Best Buy Co., Inc., a specialty retailer of consumer electronics, personal computers, entertainment software, and appliances.

Ms. Thompson was Best Buy's "organizational guru" when she learned of an experiment in Minneapolis by the company's work-life balance program manager, Cali Ressler. Together they worked to implement ROWE (Results-Only Work Environment) as a companywide program. Ms. Thompson and Ms. Ressler then founded CultureRx, a consulting company specializing in ROWE.

Ms. Thompson and Ms. Ressler are the coauthors of the upcoming book *Why Work Sucks and How You Can Fix It: Inside the Result-Only Revolution*. They have been featured in *BusinessWeek*, *HR Magazine*, the *New York Times*, and *TIME*, and on *60 Minutes* and National Public Radio.

About the Contributors

Laura Tyson is the former dean of London Business School. Currently, she is a professor at the Haas School of Business, University of California, Berkeley.

Professor Tyson joined London Business School as dean in 2002 and left that position at the end of 2006. Before that, she had been a professor of economics and business administration at the University of California.

She served in the Clinton administration from January 1993 to December 1996. Between February 1995 and December 1996 she served as the president's national economic adviser and was the highest-ranking woman in the Clinton White House.

Professor Tyson was a key architect of President Clinton's domestic and international policy agenda during his first term in office. As the administration's top economic adviser, she managed all economic policy-making throughout the executive branch.

Prior to that appointment she served as the sixteenth chairman of the White House Council of Economic Advisers, the first woman to hold that post. Before joining the Clinton administration, Professor Tyson published a number of books and articles on industrial competitiveness and trade, including the book *Who's Bashing Whom? Trade Conflict in High-Technology Industries.*

Professor Tyson has served on three boards of directors since 1997: Morgan Stanley, Eastman Kodak Co., and AT&T Inc. (formerly Ameritech Corp.).

About the Contributors

Sir Mark Weinberg is the cofounder and president of the wealth management group St. James's Place Capital.

Sir Mark has more than forty years' experience in the financial services market. In 1961 he founded Abbey Life Assurance Co. Ltd., where he formed one of the U.K.'s first property funds. Ten years later he started Hambro Life Assurance (now part of Zurich Financial Services), which grew to become the largest unit-linked life assurance company in the U.K. There he formed the first retail managed fund.

He was deputy chairman of the principal U.K. regulatory body, the Securities and Investment Board, from its inception in 1985 until 1990.

In 1991 he cofounded St. James's Place Capital plc (renamed St. James's Place in 2006) of which he remains president.

⊰ ACKNOWLEDGMENTS ⊱

First and foremost, a heartfelt thanks goes
to all of the executives who have candidly
shared their hard-earned experience and
battle-tested insights for the Lessons
Learned series.

Angelia Herrin at Harvard Business
School Publishing consistently offered un-
wavering support, good humor, and counsel from the inception of this ambitious
project.

Brian Surette, Hollis Heimbouch, and
David Goehring provided invaluable edito-
rial direction, perspective, and encourage-
ment. Much appreciation goes to Jennifer
Lynn for her research and diligent attention
to detail. Many thanks to the entire HBSP
team of designers, copy editors, and marketing professionals who helped bring this
series to life.

Finally, thanks to our fellow cofounder
James MacKinnon and the entire Fifty

Acknowledgments

Lessons team for the tremendous amount of time, effort, and steadfast support for this project.

—Adam Sodowick
   Andy Hasoon
   Directors and Cofounders
   Fifty Lessons